31-Day Plan for Overcoming Denial:
Revealing the Hidden Opportunities for Your Life - Daybook

By Angela Taylor

31-Day Plan for Overcoming Denial:
Revealing the Hidden Opportunities for Your Life
Daybook

Copyright © 2016
By Angela Taylor All rights reserved

No part of this book may be used or reproduced in any manner whatsoever without written permission except in the case of brief quotations embodied in critical articles and review. For information, address Start to Finish Publishers, P.O. Box 311, Richton Park, Illinois 60471

Start to Finish books may be purchased upon request.
Email: contact@denialanddepression.com

The first, Start to Finish paperback edition published 2016
Printed in the United States of America.

Cover Design
"Angel Wooden Queen"
By Joffrey Pavesi
www.facebook.com/JPavesiarts
E-mail: hannibawl@gmail.com

The Library of Congress has catalogued the paperback edition as follows:

Taylor, Angela, 1966-
31-Day Plan for Overcoming Denial:
Revealing the Hidden Opportunities for Your Life - Daybook

31-Day Plan for Overcoming Denial:

Revealing the Hidden Opportunities for Your Life

Daybook

This daybook was created for you to begin examining your life and uncovering the denials possibly controlling your behavior. These denials may be holding you back from moving forward and preventing you from experiencing all of the good available to you. The questions are designed to help you become aware of your denial stories and embrace your truth, which only you know.

This book is for you and only you; no one has to know about it. Place it in a safe, secure place where no one else will find it in order for you to explore your true thoughts and feelings about the situations, circumstances, and events you have experienced thus far without interference from well-meaning people who may not be able to assist you in your quest.

This book is not designed to replace a professional counselor, therapist, medical doctor, or other mental health and wellness professional. If you think you may be depressed, experiencing anxiety, or think you may need to discuss your challenges with a professional in order to sort out your life or if you think you may need medication, seek a professional to assist you. If you complete the daybook and then decide you need to seek a professional to assist you in your restoration, do so. In order to reach your destination, you must follow through with your plans.

These questions are designed for you to begin to shed light on things you are avoiding. These questions will surface your fears to inspect them and see them for what they are—challenges you need to discover a way through. Answering these questions will give your true thoughts and emotions a voice and allow you to come face-to-face with the fears/challenges keeping you from progressing, reaching goals, or changing your life.

Read my book, *The Beauty and Vanity of Denial* and its companion guide, "30 Steps for Overcoming Denial and Revealing the Hidden Opportunities for Your Life;" the book, companion guide, and the daybook are designed to inspire you to begin to ask yourself questions you may not have asked before, yet may begin to shed some light on the dark places your denials are hiding.

**These questions were not created to take the place of support from a medical, wellness, or mental health professional, therapy, or counseling of any kind. **

1. **Examine your life in its current state. Which areas from "The 8 Areas of the Circle of Life" (Body, Mental, Emotional, Relationships, Career/Lifestyle, Financial, Energy, Spiritual) do you detect stories of denial? Write down your current challenges in <u>each area</u> of the Circle of Life; focus on the emotions you feel about each challenge and why you want to change—now.**

    Example: Body: I am experiencing weight gain. I feel uncomfortable in my clothes. I feel embarrassed to eat in front of other people because I think they're judging me. I feel ashamed, frustrated, angry, and sad because I seem unable to control my eating and I don't feel motivated to exercise or increase my activity level. I want to change now because I'm fed up with feeling uncomfortable and guilty. I want to feel confident, empowered, healthy, and sexy.

    Body:

    _____
    _____
    _____
    _____
    _____
    _____
    _____
    _____
    _____

    Mental:

    _____
    _____
    _____
    _____
    _____
    _____

Emotional:

Relationships:

Finances:

_____
_____
_____
_____
_____
_____
_____

Career/Lifestyle:

_____
_____
_____
_____
_____
_____
_____
_____

Spiritual:

_____
_____
_____
_____

_____
_____
_____
_____
_____

Energy:

_____
_____
_____
_____
_____
_____
_____
_____
_____

2. **It is important to acknowledge your denials. What are you denying that keeps you from taking a step toward change, progressing, or improving in each area? Remember, no one needs to know except you.**

Body:

_____
_____
_____
_____
_____
_____
_____
_____

Mental:

_____
_____
_____
_____
_____
_____
_____
_____

Emotional:

_____

Relationships:

Finances:

Career/Lifestyle:

Spiritual:

Energy:

3. **What are the emotions you feel when you think about <u>your</u> truth? Without judging, complaining, or making excuses for what you are thinking or feeling, contemplate your feelings. It may be challenging at first because you are unaccustomed to letting your truth be heard completely without opposition. Sit and feel your emotions for as long as you can. Practice letting your truth be heard and acknowledged by you.**

Example: Body: I tell myself I'm just too stressed out to release the weight right now. When my life calms down, I will be able to release the weight.

Body:

_____
_____
_____
_____
_____
_____
_____
_____
_____

Mental:

_____
_____
_____
_____
_____
_____
_____
_____

Emotional:

Relationships:

Finances:

Career/Lifestyle:

Spiritual:

Energy:

4. **What are you trying to avoid in these areas due to fear of...a conversation; what other people may do or say; a lifestyle change; feeling overwhelming emotions; etc. Additionally, what emotions do you feel when you think about revealing your truth? Be as honest and specific as you can.**

Example: Body: I am avoiding feeling sad when I eat excessively and compulsively. The food makes me feel better for a while. When I think about revealing my truth, I feel anxious and sad because I have been trying to lose weight on my own with some success, but haven't been able to make any lasting changes. I feel too embarrassed to ask for help because I should know what to do.

Body:

_____
_____
_____
_____
_____
_____
_____
_____
_____
_____

Mental:

_____
_____
_____
_____
_____
_____
_____
_____

Emotional:

Relationships:

Finances:

Career/Lifestyle:

Spiritual:

Energy:

5. **Why aren't you living your truth? What benefits are you receiving in these areas keeping you in denial and what other options will allow you to live more authentically and result in the perks you are currently receiving?**

Example: Body: My perks are receiving the money to buy the food I need to feel better (I am currently unemployed and my spouse supports me). Other options for receiving money could be getting a job to make money, which would make me feel more empowered. Options for not feeling negative emotions that the food keep at bay would be to discuss my circumstances, thoughts, and emotions with a professional who can help me understand and manage these feelings in a more effective way

Body:

_____
_____
_____
_____
_____
_____
_____
_____
_____
_____

Mental:

_____
_____
_____
_____
_____

Emotional:

Relationships:

Finances:

_____
_____
_____
_____
_____
_____
_____
_____
_____

Career/Lifestyle:

_____
_____
_____
_____
_____
_____
_____
_____
_____

Spiritual:

_____
_____
_____
_____
_____

Energy:

6. **What would it take for you to begin to live <u>your</u> truth so that your life feels more authentic?**

   Example: *Body: I can disclose my challenges to a trusted confidant who can help me, or refer me to someone who can, or seek a professional therapist or counselor to talk with about the circumstances, thoughts, and emotions that cause me to eat excessively.*

   Body:

   _____
   _____
   _____
   _____
   _____

   Mental:

   _____
   _____
   _____
   _____
   _____

   Emotional:

   _____
   _____
   _____
   _____
   _____

   Relationships:

   _____
   _____
   _____

_____
_____

Finances:

_____
_____
_____
_____
_____

Career/Lifestyle:

_____
_____
_____
_____
_____

Spiritual:

_____
_____
_____
_____
_____

Energy:

_____
_____
_____
_____
_____

7. **Why aren't you living your truth?**

Example: Body: I believe fear of the unknown keeps me from living my truth.

Body:
_____
_____
_____
_____
_____

Mental:
_____
_____
_____
_____
_____

Emotional:
_____
_____
_____
_____
_____

Relationships:
_____
_____
_____
_____
_____

Finances:

_____
_____
_____
_____
_____

Career/Lifestyle:

_____
_____
_____
_____
_____

Spiritual:

_____
_____
_____
_____
_____

Energy:

_____
_____
_____
_____
_____

8. **What are the pros and cons of making the necessary changes to make your life feel more authentic?**

Example: Body: Pro = I will release the weight I have been trying to release. Con = I don't know what to expect. I don't like feeling uncertain.

What emotions are associated with these pros and cons?

Example: Body: The emotions I feel about releasing the weight is relief. The emotions I feel about being uncertain are anxiety and frustration.

Body:

_____
_____
_____
_____
_____

Mental:

_____
_____
_____
_____
_____

Emotional:

_____
_____
_____
_____
_____

Relationships:

_____
_____
_____
_____
_____

Finances:

_____
_____
_____
_____
_____

Career/Lifestyle:

_____
_____
_____
_____
_____

Spiritual:

_____
_____
_____
_____
_____

Energy:

_____
_____
_____
_____
_____

9. **Think creatively. What are some options that would help you move forward; possibilities you had not thought about before; people, services, programs, and/or organizations available to assist you, and likely favorable outcomes if you take action?**

Example: Body: I will schedule a physical with my doctor. I will meet with a dietician or research nutritional programs and choose and participate in a program to assist me with creating meal plans appropriate and healthy for me. I will contact the local fitness facility and hire a personal fitness trainer to design an exercise program appropriate for me to perform at home.

Body:

_____
_____
_____
_____
_____

Mental:

_____
_____
_____
_____
_____

Emotional:

_____
_____
_____
_____
_____

Relationships:

_____

Finances:

Career/Lifestyle:

Spiritual:

Energy:

10. To get where we want to be, we must go through what it will take to get there; we learn what we need in order to graduate to the next level. For what specific reasons are you not moving forward, improving, or reaching your goals in each area?

Body:

_____
_____
_____
_____
_____

Mental:

_____
_____
_____
_____
_____

Emotional:

_____
_____
_____
_____
_____

Relationships:

_____
_____
_____

Finances:

Career/Lifestyle:

Spiritual:

Energy:

11. What are you willing to feel, endure, do, say, or experience in order to feel good, be more authentic, enjoy your life, and take advantage of the new opportunities that will be open to you once you have taken action?

Body:

___

Mental:

___

Emotional:

___

Relationships:

___

Finances:

_____
_____
_____
_____
_____

Career/Lifestyle:

_____
_____
_____
_____
_____

Spiritual:

_____
_____
_____
_____
_____

Energy:

_____
_____
_____
_____
_____

12. What are you not willing to risk? Why?

Body:

_____
_____
_____
_____
_____

Mental:

_____
_____
_____
_____
_____

Emotional:

_____
_____
_____
_____
_____

Relationships:

_____
_____
_____
_____
_____

Finances:

_____
_____
_____
_____
_____

Career/Lifestyle:

_____
_____
_____
_____
_____

Spiritual:

_____
_____
_____
_____
_____

Energy:

_____
_____
_____
_____
_____

Forgiveness

It is important to forgive. Forgiving does not mean forgetting; to forgive means letting go of the past in order to move forward. In order to forgive, it is important to know certain things that may not occur to us when we are stressed or feeling intense emotions.

First, it is imperative to understand every human being makes mistakes whether or not he or she admits it. Life happens; fortunate and unfortunate things occur to <u>all</u> people no matter how good we believe we are or how bad we believe someone else may be. Pain is a part of life as well as knowing challenges and setbacks will ensue even while making progress.

When it comes to other people, it is important to know we are not responsible for other people's actions nor do we have control over their behavior toward us. Understanding that some people have mental and emotional issues that aren't always being managed well or at all is constructive; therefore, what people say or do to us is not always about us. Other people's issues are <u>not</u> our issues unless we accept them as ours.

Though it may seem unfair and as if we will never get over things when they occur, we do, and this makes us stronger—mentally and emotionally. The key is to decipher what will help us navigate through this period instead of being cemented in a moment that has passed. It is important to use what happens as opportunities for growth; working through our challenges helps us to become more resilient. When we reflect, we realize we were stronger than we thought, which builds courage for our future encounters.

Often after a traumatic or disturbing event, instead of moving through it we continue to relive it and hover in our mental and emotional energetic state due to our inability to forgive. Remember, circumstances or events are not responsible for our behavior or the condition of our life in the future. Absolution helps you to disengage this energy and gives you peace of mind to release space for positive energy to flow into your life. The longer you hold on to the past, the more challenging moving forward becomes. Let it go in order to live well.

We often believe we can get through a challenging period in our lives alone. We often experiment with ideas we think may help, but actually this keeps us in a state of limbo. If you need help getting beyond an event or period of life that is difficult for you, it may prove advantageous to find a mental health professional to assist you with your restoration.

It doesn't mean you're "crazy" because you require assistance from someone in the mental health field to assist you through this tough time. You are not alone; many people may continue doing things that prove moot and never get the real help they need. You are not one of them because you actually want to get better, change your life, and live the life you have always wanted minus the baggage and pain of the past. Everyone needs help sometimes.

Some of us assume we are the only ones who feel insecure about not knowing something we believe everybody else knows. It is important to recognize it is reasonable not to have all of the answers and it is acceptable to ask for help when needed. Many of us have awkward moments in which we occasionally say or do what is deemed "stupid." Saying or doing things we think may be rash does not mean we are senseless, but rather just uninformed, unaware of the facts, or just nervous. Give yourself a break.

Change takes time and practicing patience is important. We all have to do the work required to move to the next step; it is a process.

Without forgiveness, we are stuck in neutral. When we forgive, we give ourselves permission to begin the healing/restoration process.

13. Write down whom you need to forgive and why you need to forgive him/her/them. Remember to include yourself in this list. Practice forgiving yourself and others by reading the above as often as necessary and applying it to your situations.

Body:

_____
_____
_____
_____
_____

Mental:

_____
_____
_____
_____
_____

Emotional:

_____
_____
_____
_____
_____

Relationships:

_____
_____
_____
_____
_____

Finances:

___

___

___

___

___

Career/Lifestyle:

___

___

___

___

___

Spiritual:

___

___

___

___

___

Energy:

___

___

___

___

___

14. What are you grateful for?

Body:

_____
_____
_____
_____
_____

Mental:

_____
_____
_____
_____
_____

Emotional:

_____
_____
_____
_____
_____

Relationships:

_____
_____
_____
_____
_____

Finances:

_____

Career/Lifestyle:

Spiritual:

Energy:

15. **Begin the practice of staying aware of your thoughts and emotions. What are the stories, thoughts, and emotions in your default system keeping you in a negative or confused state of mind? Are you holding on to some hurt from the past? If so, refer back to question number 13 and what you have written.**

   Body:

   _____
   _____
   _____
   _____
   _____

   Mental:

   _____
   _____
   _____
   _____
   _____

   Emotional:

   _____
   _____
   _____
   _____
   _____

   Relationships:

   _____
   _____
   _____
   _____
   _____

Finances:

_____
_____
_____
_____
_____

Career/Lifestyle:

_____
_____
_____
_____
_____

Spiritual:

_____
_____
_____
_____
_____

Energy:

_____
_____
_____
_____
_____

16. Write down effective affirmations that oppose your negative self-talk and inspire you to continue moving forward.

Example: Body: Every cell in my body is healthy. Every system in my body is running at optimal capacity because I feed them the nutrition that they need and engage in the health promoting activities that my body requires to stay healthy.

Body:
_____
_____
_____
_____
_____

Mental:
_____
_____
_____
_____
_____

Emotions:
_____
_____
_____
_____
_____

Relationships:
_____
_____

___

___

___

Finances:

___

___

___

___

___

Career/Lifestyle:

___

___

___

___

___

Spiritual:

___

___

___

___

___

Energy:

___

___

___

___

___

17. Research books, movies, and documentaries that may uplift and inspire you to continue on your journey out of denial. Look at the list of books and documentaries listed in the *Beauty and Vanity of Denial* that may help you.

1. _____
2. _____
3. _____
4. _____
5. _____
6. _____

18. What do you want your life to <u>look</u> and <u>feel</u> like in each area of the Circle of Life?

Body:

_____
_____
_____
_____
_____

Mental:

_____
_____
_____
_____
_____

Emotions:

_____
_____
_____
_____
_____

Relationships:

_____
_____
_____
_____
_____

Finances:

_____
_____
_____
_____
_____

Career/Lifestyle:

_____
_____
_____
_____
_____

Spiritual:

_____
_____
_____
_____
_____

Energy:

_____
_____
_____
_____
_____

19. What does an ordinary day in your future look and feel like to you in each area of the Circle of Life? Using your imagination, what activities are you involved in and what people or groups do you socialize with from the time you wake up until you go to bed? Be as specific as you can by utilizing as many details as you can.

Body:

_____
_____
_____
_____
_____

Mental:

_____
_____
_____
_____
_____

Emotions:

_____
_____
_____
_____
_____

Relationships:

_____
_____
_____
_____
_____

Finances:

_____
_____
_____
_____
_____

Career/Lifestyle:

_____
_____
_____
_____
_____

Spiritual:

_____
_____
_____
_____
_____

Energy:

_____
_____
_____
_____
_____

20. **Are there specific things in your future that seem far-fetched, unreasonable, and unlikely for you? What are they? Why do you have doubts? After careful consideration, are your doubts real or imagined?**

_____
_____
_____
_____
_____
_____
_____
_____
_____

21. **Have you ever meditated for relaxation or spiritual connection? If so, what benefits did you receive from the practice? Are you still practicing? If no, what other form(s) of relaxation are you currently practicing, consistently? How does it help you or what are the drawbacks?**

_____
_____
_____
_____
_____

22. What methods of relaxation or spiritual connection would you like to learn more about and practice? Do the research to find out where they are located, their contact information, and schedule. Schedule and attend the class, seminar, lecture, or workshop appropriate for you. Write down your experiences with each one.

1. _____
2. _____
3. _____
4. _____
5. _____

_____
_____
_____
_____
_____
_____
_____
_____
_____
_____
_____
_____
_____
_____
_____
_____
_____

23. Are you currently exercising or actively engaged in a fitness program that you participate in consistently? What do you do for exercise? If you do not exercise, what stops you?

_____
_____
_____
_____
_____
_____
_____
_____
_____
_____

24. Plan a course of action. What is the first step you are going to take to lead to feeling better, being better, and living better? What is your plan B?

_____
_____
_____
_____
_____
_____
_____
_____
_____
_____

25. **Write down each step that you will take in your plan.**

Step 1:

_____

_____

_____

_____

_____

_____

Step 2:

_____

_____

_____

_____

_____

_____

Step 3:

_____

_____

_____

_____

_____

_____

Step 4:

_____

_____

_____

26. Which step(s) in your action plan requires assistance?

27. What type of assistance do you need in each area (planning, people, organizations, doctors, groups, etc.)? What is your plan B?

Body:

_____
_____
_____
_____
_____

Mental:

_____
_____
_____
_____
_____

Emotions:

_____
_____
_____
_____
_____

Relationships:

_____
_____
_____
_____
_____

Finances:

_____
_____
_____
_____
_____

Career/Lifestyle:

_____
_____
_____
_____
_____

Spiritual:

_____
_____
_____
_____
_____

Energy:

_____
_____
_____
_____
_____

28. Research and write down the information (names, addresses, phone numbers, etc.) for the assistance you need (friends, family members, organizations, therapist, therapy group, doctors, spiritual counselor, family counselor, mentor etc.).

Body:

_____
_____
_____
_____
_____

Mental:

_____
_____
_____
_____
_____

Emotional:

_____
_____
_____
_____
_____

Relationships:

_____
_____
_____
_____
_____

Finances:

_____
_____
_____
_____
_____

Career/Lifestyle:

_____
_____
_____
_____
_____

Spiritual:

_____
_____
_____
_____
_____

Energy:

_____
_____
_____
_____
_____

29. Make contact with the assistance you need in each area. Schedule an appointment or meeting. Note results.

Body:

_____
_____
_____
_____
_____

Mental:

_____
_____
_____
_____
_____

Emotional:

_____
_____
_____
_____
_____

Relationships:

_____
_____
_____
_____
_____

Finances:

___

Career/Lifestyle:

___

Spiritual:

___

Energy:

___

30. Develop/find a support group to help you continue moving forward. Who are the people in your support group and what is their contact information?

1. _____
2. _____
3. _____
4. _____
5. _____

31. What lifestyle changes will become your new normal way of living free from denial? Choose changes promoting authenticity, joy, relaxation, peace of mind, orderliness, harmony, wellness, and will keep you physically active and engaged in healthy behaviors!

_____
_____
_____
_____
_____
_____

For additional information visit:
www.BeautyAndVanity.com
www.DenialAndDepression.com
or email Angela at:
Angela@BeautyAndVanity.com
contact@DenialAndDepression.com